52 SOLAR PANELS

Love and Grief for a Son and a Planet

JOHN MOORHEAD-GUINEA

Copyright © 2022 John Moorhead-Guinea
All rights reserved.

ISBN 978-2-9701649-0-6

No part of this publication may be reproduced, distributed, or transmitted in any form or by any means, including photocopying, recording, or other electronic or mechanical methods, or by any information storage and retrieval system without the prior written permission of the publisher, except in the case of very brief quotations embodied in critical reviews and certain other noncommercial uses permitted by copyright law.

Editor: Anita Verna Crofts
Photograph: Oskar Hall
Publishing assistance: The Writing House

Dedicated to mountain guides, rescue, ski patrols and all those that keep us safe in the mountains.

Alps

Jagged teeth against
crisp blue air,
the glacier receding

White blanket lifting
Greys, greens, yellows, reds gaining
Gaining too, guilty greedy humans
and their machines
Losing: the playful, joyful, the innocent, nature
those that climb, hike, ski, love nature

As the great warming smothers, so does
the soot-black smoke,
the all-grey rock and clouds,
the frothing mountains of white-water and ash
that flow into the valley

As the mountain, so the glacier, trees keel over,
flowers wither and dry into dust
The Chamois surprised by the striking rock,
falls

Preface

In 2021, I lost my son Alex.

Alex was the best a dad could possibly dream of. He was loving, caring, and selfless. He brought people together and encouraged harmony rather than division and argument. He brought laughter and joy to his family and friends.

When Alex died, I was working on a book about scaling up regenerative climate solutions that work in harmony with nature. However, what you are holding in your hands is a letter.

I paused the book and wrote this letter and poems to Alex out of love for him and our family. I wish to honor him and treasure my memories of him. I meditate on how love and grief can be channeled to climate action that preserves nature and saves human lives.

This letter recasts climate and environmental action as a matter of the heart. It combines the action Alex was pursuing with mine. It's my way of keeping Alex by my side in the only labor I know, making it a labor of love.

December 19, 2021

Dear Alex,

Our first night home with you from the hospital in Mexico City did not go well. You cried and cried, so much so that we called the pediatrician at 3:00 in the morning. Thankfully, you fell asleep soon thereafter.

But despite this rough start, I was besotted. You fascinated me. My first-born son, now home!

I spent hours watching you, holding you, and filming you with our newly acquired camcorder (asleep or not). I wanted to be with you all the time.

Proving that first night at home was an anomaly, you became such a happy baby. You slept and ate so well.

Deirdre, you and I lived in an L-shaped bungalow with white walls and a red terracotta roof, surrounded by birds-of-paradise and a meticulously kept lawn. The life-filled chaos of Mexico City lapped at our closed street entrance.

You were a blonde novelty. Locals wanted to touch your head as if touching a blonde baby's head brought luck. I knew I was the luckiest of all.

When you were only three weeks old, we flew to Geneva so my parents could meet you. For your Mexican passport, the official needed you to open your eyes for the photograph, but you were fast asleep. They stayed closed and the photograph is of you, sleeping.

You loved the water and beach, all covered up to protect you from the sun, with a hat like a desert legionnaire.

Time flew.

We moved back to Switzerland in 1997, a year after you were born. Your brother Nick was born in 1998 months later in March and your sister Emeline two years after that in 2000.

We did not just play at happy families, we really were happy. Your hiding place was tucked inside three pine trees growing closely together. You spoke a secret language, *Lagenbagen*. You had "days off" with your grandparents at their home in a village nestled in the Jura's shadow in nearby France.

In the winter from the hedge at the top of the garden, we would pile up snow. I pushed your blue plastic sled off the hedge onto the sled run, patted down for speed, all the way to the bottom hedge. We went skiing on weekdays and weekends in the Jura and in Verbier for the longer holidays. Your little skis went over my right ski on the button tow.

In the summer we swam in our unheated old mountain pool. The season was short because we lived at mid-mountain altitude on the Jura. Over the years it became warmer earlier in the season, and we could celebrate your June birthday on a couple of occasions by the pool. We spent summer holidays on Cape Cod in Massachusetts, in Maine, and Hondarribia, on the US and Spanish sides of the Atlantic: Deirdre and my childhood summer places.

You simply loved to be outside. You were a happy, easy-going, and loving child who rarely got angry or cried. Your first day at school was so very hard for Deirdre and me. You clutched your snowman *nene* as we said our *au revoir* through the narrow rectangular window.

But you liked going to school. You loved playing football and skiing. You were an amazing goalie. As you were not the tallest you learned to jump faster and further than the others, like a steel spring coiled taut and suddenly released.

Thanks to nearby Jura ski resorts your skiing got better and better and you loved to jump off hills and over rocks. On school ski days I could take you with your classmates through the woods. It was a grand adventure!

You were so much fun to be with. I loved reading stories to you, the best ones that we invented together. Sometimes they worked, sometimes they did not. Either way, we enjoyed the telling.

Time flew by even faster.

When you turned ten, you joined the International School of Geneva. All three of you were at the same school, as thick as thieves at home and in play, bouncing down ever steeper slopes. You learned to climb, also in the Jura initially, and it was to become your second passion, after skiing.

Your fierce loyalty to your friends sometimes conflicted with your honesty. You had to make some hard choices. You said that an imitation gun was yours when it was not. For this you had to appear in juvenile court. I was so proud of you for taking the rap for those who were less confident or too fearful to do so. I was there with you at juvenile court.

I could not be with you at the International School of Geneva the day they interrogated you and decided to expel you. All I could do was to take you straight to the Swiss public school to be admitted the day after your expulsion. You were unfairly treated by some at the International School when you had the courage to choose honesty over loyalty. You were expelled by one headmaster but readmitted by another at the International School. You made so many good friends whether at Swiss public or international schools. People trusted you.

You were already saving lives as a youngster. At a party when somebody you did not know got severely intoxicated you got his parents' phone number and made sure he was taken care of, staying with him until they came to pick him up.

After renting a place in Verbier during the winter ski holidays we began renting for the whole of the winter season, going there for every day off, weekend, and holiday possible.

We all loved skiing, powder-skiing most of all. You became a freeride skier. Your mom and I took you to freeride competitions all over Europe and to the US for the World Junior Freeride championship. It was so much fun to discover new ski resorts. We loved to watch you ski, as you were such a fluid, graceful and beautiful skier. You loved to ski for yourself and with your friends, but to compete, not so much.

You did well at school and chose to take a gap year before university. You mastered German in Berlin, spent a month apprenticing with a cheese maker, helped in a Peruvian rainforest, and worked in a ski shop in Verbier. You became independent, renting your first apartment in Fribourg to attend university.

You always had work, whether in a ski shop, for the Swiss railways, as a ski patroller, or at the tourist office maintaining mountain trails. You studied environmental sciences at the University of Lausanne. You made more friends. We loved you for who you were and who you were becoming: a truly wonderful young man, confident in yourself, responsible, sensitive, and caring.

In a world of selfishness, greed, and entitlement you stood out as somebody who was generous, selfless, humble, shy, and unassuming. You did not judge. You had a great sense of humor and were very good at the local Valaisan accent.

You were at home in so many different settings, speaking English, French, Spanish fluently and German and Italian with such ease. You accepted and were easily accepted because you were so sensitive and did not criticize.

You were most at home in the mountains.

As much as you enjoyed freeride skiing you also loved ski-touring and climbing mountains. You became so good at climbing that you were admitted to be a Swiss mountain guide. As with your skiing, you were always very careful, responsible, and meticulous. You did not take unnecessary risks and stayed within your capabilities. You climbed when it was safest to do so.

You were building your life project around the mountains you loved so much. I did not see much of you in the last year of your life. You were so busy with mountaineering, ski patrol, and working in Anzère in the summer.

I knew that you were loved by so many and that you were in such a good place. I did not think anything could happen to you, Alex.

June 6, 2022

On October 19, 2021, you were killed by falling rocks as you climbed the Matterhorn.

Such a rockfall is a very rare occurrence, the odds of which have worsened due to human-caused climate change.

It was a freak accident that happened because you were in the right place at the wrong time. It should have never happened, but it did.

Alex, you loved and are loved and missed by your family and friends, the pain forever.

How is it possible that you lost your life that day?

The conditions were ideal for climbing the Matterhorn for weeks before and after your climb. You did everything right on the day and consulted extensively with experienced guides before the climb. Experienced guides told me that it could have been them that day and that they could not have done anything to avoid being killed.

The rockfall that killed you was a rare event, and yet, on that day, one-in-six climbing parties never came back alive from the north face of the Matterhorn.

I think of you and miss you every day. My love for you is unending. My mind and heart feel incomplete without you.

Losing you gave my life added urgency. What could I do with my consuming grief, whose origins were that of deep love for you? While it is unthinkable to see your death as anything other than a tragedy, I wish to channel my emotions in ways that befit you and the mountains you so loved. This appreciation for the natural world is something that we shared and that I can act on.

My intention is not just to write a book about losing you and what words may bring comfort to those overwhelmed by grief. As a climate activist and researcher, I am also writing a book about the relationship between love and the most existential threat to humanity and nature: human-induced climate change. My book project, originally on how to scale up regenerative climate solutions, began when you were alive, and it continues now after your death.

But I am a changed man, and my new perspective is one I must share.

Loving you was deeply transformative, as was losing you. It has sharpened my focus and shifted my thinking on the relationship between love and saving this planet we call home. This Earth that we cannot afford to lose.

We refer to "losing a loved one" for a reason. Love for each other, ourselves, nature, and earth is what saves us. When you lose a loved one you need to find new ways to express your love for whom you lost and those who remain. Family and friends have expressed their love for me and mine to them in the wake of your death, Alex. Love that we took for granted comes pouring out. It is all that is left.

It is time for all of us to express our love, now more than ever. Not just because of our own mortality, but because each act of love can contribute to a world restored.

July 19, 2022

A year before your death, our family had moved to live all-year-round in the Swiss Alps village of Le Châble, in the valley below Verbier, to be closer to nature and the outdoor activities we love: skiing, hiking, and climbing. We are a close-knit family that loves the outdoors.

You and your friends became our impromptu moving company, filling and emptying our rented van. All our furniture was strewn on the street, as if we were going to live outdoors, but then was quickly carried into our new home, a high-ceilinged apartment with bright red shutters and a sunny kitchen. There was excitement in the air as your mountaineering and skiing friends pitched in. We were reunited in the mountains.

You were already living in a village close to Anzère, working as a ski patroller during the winter. You came to skiers' rescue with the red rescue wooden luge behind you, like an unwieldy caravan. During the summer you took care of mountain hiking routes by clearing trails, building wooden bridges, and refreshing the red and white paint on rocks. You repaired the distinctive yellow signs that point you in the right direction and tell you that you are in Switzerland. You were often the first on and last off the mountain.

You were an extremely able and experienced alpinist that climbed scores of towering peaks in

Switzerland, Italy, and France. You completed your first climbing course at age ten. You always had an athletic build that allowed you to lift your body off the ground with your hands with ease.

In the last few years of your life, Alex, you had been doing more and more demanding climbing. You were so capable that you were accepted to the prestigious Swiss Mountain Guide program. Your course instructor was so impressed with your ability that he shared a video he had taken of you and explained that you had the *pied montagnard* translated to "mountain foot" or sure-footedness. This was a rare compliment to bestow upon a 25-year-old by an alpinist who had climbed the Matterhorn for many years.

Last November at the Swiss Mountain Guide orientation your chair was empty.

A few days before your death, you shared with us the wonderful news that you were to start a new job as a project manager at a Swiss avalanche detection and management company in November. You had found a beautiful sun-bleached restored small wooden barn, to live in near Anzère. You were over-the-moon happy.

You were also a climate activist, having participated in climate marches, occupied a coal mine in Germany, and launched a sticker campaign to place on billboards of climate-disrupting-products such as gas guzzlers and beef. "Bad for both your health and that of our planet" the stickers read in French.

52 Solar Panels

As a family, our climate activism developed in different ways. From a young age, you took public transport and were part of carpools to go to and from school. Our diet became increasingly plant-based. This was not always an easy choice for you, Alex, particularly in mountain huts. As a family we had Swiss train passes, for several years, that we used to get around. For your climbing you sometimes had no choice but to take the small old green Volkswagen that the Sumoroks gave you, and which you shared with friends and family. You were engaged when it came to climate action. We went together to climate strike marches in Geneva.

You had a real eye for photography and film. In elementary school you won a printer through a photography competition, and that further launched your love of capturing life on film. Later your ski and mountaineering photographs were published in magazines and as a teenager you took first prize in the Verbier Freeride video competition. I was prouder of this achievement than you were. You were just having fun with your camera. Other artistic pursuits included playing a mean guitar, for fun.

You skied with confident intensity, entering competitions that had you navigating cliffs and *couloirs* with ease. You were not a reckless skier, but rather, a joyful one. The mountain was not something to be conquered but something with which you could commune.

I also find the mountains to be wonderful company.

The focus of my work is on regenerative climate solutions to avert climate and natural disasters. Regenerative refers to solutions that are in harmony with nature, that do not harm human health, and enable Earth to return to equilibrium and a stable climate by ending and reversing global warming. Examples of regenerative solutions include renewable energy, building with timber, and farming techniques that mimic nature's ecosystems and do not use synthetic inputs.

But now after your death, I am a world away from where I was. I still believe in the existing regenerative solutions to solve the planet from climate catastrophe. But now my grief and love make me feel differently about new strategies to scale solutions.

Losing you and your love made me center love as the only way to save us from ourselves and Earth from climate apocalypse.

Why?

Because if we truly love and care for each other and the world we inhabit, we will do what it takes to save ourselves and our families. To channel that boundless love, we must understand what saves lives, what preserves human health and nature, and what must be done about pollution to prevent the climate crisis spiraling out of control to a barren Earth.

September 20, 2022

Since your death, we have had a winter with much less snow in the Alps and sands from the Sahara that turned the snow an ugly beige. A glacier collapsed and killed eleven in the Italian Alps during a hot and dry summer. Mountain guides decided to not climb certain routes on the Jungfrau, Matterhorn, and Mont Blanc at times during the summer due to the higher risk of rockfall.

On September 11 Emeline was on a climb with your good friend Guillaume when rockfall caused massive injuries to his leg. The climb was to be a first and to honor you, Alex, for a new route you had helped open at the Miroir d'Argentine.

The mountains are becoming more unstable, and some alpine risks are going up due to warmer temperatures and more extreme weather events, made worse by human climate change.

Throughout the world human-induced climate change and pollution are contributing to the death of millions of loved ones. Families are losing loved ones to more frequent and devastating natural disasters such as floods, landslides, or fires and extreme weather events such as heatwaves and storms, made worse by human climate change.

My grief for you has galvanized me. I now advocate for love to save humanity from the climate catastrophe we are marching towards.

My mission helps me put a floor under my depthless grief.

In your before-last birthday card to me, you wrote that I was your hero for "trying to save the planet." It has been my later life's work, this is true. But Alex, you are the hero for following your passions and convictions.

How you led your life inspires me every day to move forward and lifts my heart.

You helped so many through your selfless love. Those who did not know you well have since told me the positive feeling they had after meeting you, even briefly.

October 1, 2022

When my life came crashing down in a gut-wrenching whirlwind of sadness, fear, loneliness, disbelief, guilt, anxiety, anger, and regret, the one emotion that came to my rescue is love. Love for and by our families, friends, and for nature is what saved me when I lost you.

Those who showed love for me, as well as long walks in nature, sunsets and sunrises are what I remember in the months following your death. These forms of care helped me get through the endless nightmare of losing you.

Love is affection, selflessness, generosity, honesty, taking responsibility, sharing with, and caring for others. Love means leading a life that does not harm. It is the most important human emotion for our wellbeing and that of our planet.

You showed your love in ways that serve as examples.

To start, you put others' lives before yours. As a ski patroller, you rescued skiers in the winters and in the summers, you made mountain itineraries safe for hikers and worked at mountain huts that provide shelter to hikers. Your goal was to be a mountain guide to help others, less able than yourself, enjoy the mountains. You extended what you loved to as many people as possible, rather than hoard it all for yourself.

Much of the climate crisis is due to selfish behavior and greed. Being selfless is an important trait to prevent human climate change and help others when climate change disrupts lives. Selflessness also inclines you to help others who are most vulnerable.

You expressed your love in so many ways and did so quietly and with humility. You accepted people for who they were, hated confrontation, and liked to bring people together rather than argue and divide. I remember family meals when I was argumentative. You would raise your eyebrows and a troubled look would cross your face, but you would remain silent rather than argue.

Your curiosity made you wise and mature beyond your age. You were equally comfortable learning about environmental sciences at university and while in the mountains you climbed. You absorbed so much about their structure, geology, how they were formed, how they were being affected by climate change, that you quickly became very knowledgeable. Your undergraduate thesis was on how the precipitation patterns are changing the Swiss Alps.

Collaboration, openness, impartiality, and understanding the science and its application are so important to solving the climate crisis, and you had them all.

You practiced what you shared with others: to do no harm. You led an honest and responsible life.

. . .

You biked everywhere, once joining us in Antibes from Switzerland—hundreds of kilometers away—by bike, with Emeline. Your jobs involved working for Swiss trains, maintaining pedestrian trails and as a mountain hut guardian. You adopted a plant-based diet as circumstances would allow. These are activities that do no or much less harm than many others and have to do with a life of being closer to nature. You thought and practiced how you could do the least harm possible (using the car rarely, not wasting food). You were the king of leftovers in Tupperware!

You denounced consumption and waste by tagging billboards of wasteful and environmentally damaging products. You wanted nothing to do with a society that equates money and consumption with happiness. You were a reluctant shopper except when it came to your equipment for skiing and climbing. You did not want to work in an office and have a career in the traditional private or public sector. You wanted to live and let live, without harm to others, in the mountains.

To lead a life rich in experiences not possessions could have been your slogan. Your values and how you led your life inspires me on how I want to lead my own.

So how do I love you now that you are gone? You were such an important part of my life and now you have vanished forever. How do I restore my equilibrium?

One way is to increase my effort to restore the equilibrium of the earth. An important part of showing my unending love for you is to have that love mirror my love for the earth and the humans and nature that inhabit it. You channeled your concern as a climate activist. By combining your activism with mine, I show my love for you and the earth you were so fortunate to inhabit. While you could not save your own life or the lives of countless others, you would have if you could.

October 15, 2022

Your love for the mountains and for your family and friends continues to inspire me. Indeed, it has had me rethink the entire framework of my book. Because when you cast climate action in terms of love, it changes how we think about solutions

For example, it feels good to walk or bike to school, to work, or for leisure. To walk to catch a bus, subway, or train to get to our destination also feels good. Our bodies become fitter; our minds become clearer. You knew this, Alex, as you practiced it from a young age. Furthermore, by going car-free or sharing a car we show our love for human life.

We know that cars pollute the air we breathe and that this ends our lives earlier. Too many of us die or are maimed as defenseless pedestrians, or cyclists hit by cars and trucks. We are also dying in gruesome car accidents, either behind the wheel or as a passenger.

But there is another path we can take. A path I am more determined than ever to walk and share with others because of you. What would a choice look like led by love?

To start, we need not fall for the marketed easy lie of cars equating freedom. We need not buy into the car advertisements of one person driving one car on an empty winding mountain road alone.

We need not aspire to be trapped in a car with thousands of others in their cars and trucks on a superhighway on a beautiful warm spring day.

Instead, if we make the choice to own a car, we can share it (and plan for the next to be no car at all, an electric bike or electric car). Co-ownership is an act of love. By sharing we show care for others. We reduce the number of cars and car journeys. This reduces the heat which warms our ocean waters. The hurricanes that will inevitably form will be less powerful and will displace or kill fewer humans and destroy fewer buildings once they hit land. Think also of those whose lives would have been saved rather than lost to a mudslide, collapsing cliff, heatwave, fire, or flood.

Our loved ones and our planet simply can no longer afford a billion cars sitting on driveways, parking lots, and streets. These machines sit there idle, boiling hot in the summer, often useless and ugly. Cars fill our physical space until their owner turns up to convey them from A to B, often solo driving. The hot asphalt they sit on smothers precious soil and nature that instead could have yielded trees, flowers and nature's bounty of fruits, nuts, and vegetables. What a waste.

We also know that too little or too much food shortens millions of lives. We die because of malnourishment from insufficient healthy food and access to clean water. We die earlier from heart disease, diabetes, and cancer due to too much meat (particularly red meat) and over-processed food. We die from too much sugar, salt, and fat in food that is highly processed. We also die from insufficient fruits, nuts, and vegetables in our diet.

We need not fall for the marketed convenience of fast food and drinks all wrapped in throwaway plastic. We will not let our bodies fall prey to the salt-sugar-fat-laden traps (and their armada of synthetic chemical substitutes) set by processed and ultra-processed foods. Nor will we fall for the lie of cheap meat produced at the expense of millions of humans' health and lives, forests mowed down to feed cows, and agriculture that feeds animals rather than humans.

Alternatively, those of us that eat too much meat and dairy can switch to a far more plant-based tasty diet. It is an act of love to eat less meat for our own health. This can quickly halve the 1.5 billion cattle that so destructively live on our planet. Land is freed up for agriculture for humans and rainforests can be preserved. Nature is restored. You knew this all too well, Alex, as you embraced a plant-based diet.

The heatwaves, droughts, and forest fires become less destructive. They kill fewer humans and burn less nature and wildlife. Less of our precious water is used up by cows' up to 250 liters a day water habit.

It's up to us to connect the dots between how we live and millions of acts of love and kindness that we can choose to make to preserve loved ones' precious lives.

October 22, 2022

A year after your death, Mom, Nick, Emeline, and I are following different paths in how we grieve you. I know that you would have liked us to carry on with our lives. You did not like fuss. However, we love you so much and are so heartbroken that our lives are forever changed. We are finding new paths. We continue to hike, bike, walk, ski, and spend time in nature because that's what we did, what continues to help us live. Emeline became a ski instructor during the winter and mountain bike teacher in the summer. She has started University again at Neuchâtel, studying biology. Nick hiked the *Tour du Mount Blanc*, he hitch-hikes everywhere, and he plays chess, including chess tournaments all over Europe. As I write, he is in Romania hiking the 1,400 kilometer *Via Transilvanica* trail, after hitchhiking north of the Arctic Circle where he hiked the 400 kilometer King's Trail in Sweden. As for me, I hike, walk, and bike every day I can, I travel, I skied last winter season as much as I could, and I am writing the book this letter introduces.

I want to help all of us—friends, family, the broader community—as we grieve you. Therefore, I am writing about my grief. To share with everyone how I grieve your loss. My hope is that by sharing my experience it can shed light on both the human condition and how we might channel what it means to be human to climate solutions that are regenerative.

Thanks to mom I have been reading books about grief, the best of which are written by those that have experienced grief firsthand either of a lost spouse or lost child. Their advice helps me. The short of it is that the pain is forever, that grief should be embraced not rejected, and that love for the dead and living is what helps us move forward rather than move on.

Losing you is the very worst that has ever happened to me. It changed me and my life forever. Friends, acquaintances, complete strangers, and family can make a big difference in how I live and move forward with my grief and sadness. Our close friends Duncan and Lindsey have held Deirdre and me close to them, in our pain, from the day you died.

While not the same as losing a loved one, friends and family are also experiencing a different form of grief: climate grief. Climate grief is grieving climate and nature that no longer exists. It is grieving the wood that burnt down, the river that has dried up, or the wildlife that no longer lives in the river that you used to walk along. It is grief for the natural world that we are an integral part of. It is grief for a stable climate that nurtured life. While a distinct kind of grief, how we collectively shoulder a new reality and move forward applies to climate grief.

Seeing your friends and family grieve is painful, Alex, and it is made more painful by my own grief.

Grief confronts us with the impermanence of human life and our own mortality. Grief is about fear, love, and compassion all at the same time. It is little wonder that we are at a complete loss particularly when it comes to the sudden death of a child as young as you, whose life was cut short eight months before your twenty-sixth birthday.

What to say to the family and friends to try to bring comfort?

Social convention provides us with a whole series of expressions such as "Sorry for your loss," "My deepest condolences," or "You are in our thoughts, prayers." We need these just as we need to greet and bid goodbye when we meet one another. But it's what you say or do after or before what convention dictates that helps grief.

"There are no words."

Maybe not. One may not be able to come up with any. But we should all try. I wish people would say something about you, Alex. If they did not know you well enough just saying an impression of who you were or what they heard about you is enough. What may feel inadequate will mean the world to me.

If friends can't say anything, they can always give me a hug, write, send me a poem or a photograph, paint a picture, donate on your behalf, or whatever way they choose to express themselves. Bringing you up is not going to hurt me anymore than I already am. Acknowledging my grief is better than ignoring it.

Your death turned the many friends that loved you grief-stricken. Your friends from neighborhoods where we lived, your schools and universities, the mountaineering and skiing community, friends and family in Ireland, Spain, UK, US, Switzerland, Germany, Sweden and beyond miss you and think of you. My friends are often at a loss how to approach me, what to say, and how to grieve your loss themselves.

I have found that for the few friends that have lost family at a young age they can relate to what I am going through and express their grief and love more easily. For them, but also those that have not, I want to help them navigate their grief and help our family, Alex.

I feel like telling them to make the unthinkable thinkable. To ask themselves: How would I feel if I lost my child or a sibling? I want to ask them to think how sad, lonely, and scared they would feel. To think of the terrible thoughts that they would have: the feelings of guilt, reliving your death in a seemingly endless loop as I do.

I then want to ask them to think about their favorite place in nature. A beloved lake or pond. Or flower. Perhaps an animal. Now imagine all traces of that treasured place or creature disappears, I would tell them. Perhaps not overnight, but unequivocally. They should take the necessary time to think and feel how they would feel, whatever time it takes to do so. Think of moments in their life when they were saddest, I would like to add. How did they feel then, what helped them most? What helped them live with their sadness?

The idea is that by using personal experience and imagination we can help each other more and better. We are each of us on different grieving paths as I mentioned earlier. So, the more we adapt our help to our personal paths the better. You were such a kind, sensitive, selfless soul that I know that you would have liked that.

To grieve you I need to be with close friends and family and on the move. Being in nature, going on long walks, skiing, admiring art, being close to a lake, the ocean and mountains, being in Spain (you were alive when I finally got my Spanish citizenship) and writing to you brings a measure of comfort to my pain

Our grief is made more complicated by climate grief, Alex. Being in nature is such an important balm of the grieving process that if we must grieve for nature at the same time, it can be painfully overwhelming. Therefore, preserving nature and helping nature's regeneration helps our grief as well as our climate grief. I seek out being in nature. If I cannot be in nature I suffer more. I express my love to you by helping nature, so that nature can help me heal and help others live.

Friends and family have been such an important presence, if not physically then virtually, and no message is too small. I will never forget how the whole of the Anzère ski patrol team joined us a year ago for the ceremony to honor and remember you. We celebrated your life that crisp sunny afternoon at the Marmottes on Savoleyres mountain. Emeline and Nick took off from the top of Savoleyres in paragliders with two of your close friends and landed near to where we were assembled, drinking white wine, photos of you clipped onto clothes lines. We clung to each other on the mountainside and would have stayed longer but the dusk and cold meant we had to leave.

We have lived through the first birthdays without you and the 19th of each month is yet another month that marks your absence. I have been on the move going to Italy, France, Spain, and the US. I have visited old friends that have welcomed me in their homes. I have shared my grief and they have with me of their lost loved ones. I have been to graves of friends who died recently and a friend who died younger than you. There is so much love, grief, and empathy for each other that I was not aware of until you died.

I have been where we spent holidays together in Maine, on Cape Cod, Hondarribia, the small fishing Basque village where Spain's Bay of Biscay coast meets France at a right angle, Madrid, and Peron in the French Jura where you spent so many happy times with your grandparents. Gerry was Police Constable Plopps, remember? You were supposed to follow his orders when it was time to go to bed.

Each time I travel, I must come back home. We call this re-entry. Re-entry does not get easier with time.

Since your death I feel vulnerable, lonely, pained, and scared. I find that "How are you doing?" is a hard question for me to answer. So, I don't. I talk about what I am doing instead with my grief, such as taking long walks or writing. I feel like telling my friends to ask me "What are you doing?" as an opening question and the "How are you doing?" can come later where we can share our feelings in an environment where I feel safe, usually one-on-one.

I have a heightened sense of awareness about who can help me and who cannot. Who feels empathy, and who does not. I can sense selfishness, insensitivity, insincerity, and lack of compassion from a mile away. So, one might as well come clean, as some friends have with me. An acquaintance of mine confessed to being selfish and the ensuing conversation was a much easier one. Another friend that feared his lack of compassion would be unhelpful, instead connected me to his wife who was one of the most compassionate people I have ever met.

I do not know what to think about friends talking about what your life could have been. I think it depends on what they refer to. If it's to say something about you that rests so clearly on who you were, then maybe. If it's not, then perhaps not. If it helps friends and family grieve, it's probably the right thing to do.

I have found that my grief for you is not linear. It can hit me out of the blue. I can be on a train looking at the passing countryside and a wave of intense sadness overwhelms me. I cry. Sometimes there are obvious triggers, sometimes not. It can be months after and I expect years after will be the same. But time is the ultimate healing source until my own death. And then others can grieve me. "This too shall pass" as the saying goes.

In the past I have used deadlines to get work done. As tempting as it may be to have a deadline by when my grief will end, it does not work that way, I have found. It's how I decide to live beyond my grief, pain, and sadness that's the key. Nor is grief something you park in your mind "to be attended to later" like a course you will take or a new language you want to learn. My grief for you needs to be confronted without being solved. It needs to be carefully navigated, neither letting myself be completely overwhelmed by it nor completely ignoring or suppressing it. Grief needs tending just as a garden does.

Friends and family can make all the difference in tending to my grief. Friends that are there for me for the long-haul help most, I am finding. Friends that offered to host me in their homes have been very patient with me and I have stayed at friends' homes in the US, Spain, France, and Italy, accepting offers months after they were made.

I can no longer plan or make decisions as I used to, Alex. I am living much more day by day and week by week. To think further than a week or two is difficult, almost painful. The one exception has to do with the climate. We are putting 52 solar panels (one for each week in a year without you) on the roof of our old chalet in Arzier, our home where you were raised, now adorned by photos by you and of you.

To mark the one-year anniversary since your death, family and friends gathered to plant a beautiful *Chaemaecyparis* tree in our garden in Arzier. Family and friends also gathered at the St. Christophe chapel above Verbier where a beautiful rock inscribed with your name sits.

My grief for you and living with sadness has taken on a central role of my remaining life. There is no point in trying to "get over you" or to "move on" from your death. It is better for me to learn to live with my sadness and grief and to channel my love for you into my writing and activism.

November 4, 2022

I was transformed twice, first when you came into my life and then when you left it.

The twenty-five years I shared with you I cherish more than I can adequately express, your love and joy irreplaceable. Those years gave me purpose and meaning. As the world was struggling for its very survival, I always thought that at least I had you as a pillar that I could anchor the rest of my life to. You understood me and filled my heart with love!

Now that you are gone, I am unmoored, and I must stay on the move like a shark that needs to swim lest it sink and die at the bottom of the ocean, its fins cut off. But how you led your life is providing me with the regenerated fins I need to keep going.

Your death broke the hearts of so many of us, friends and family alike. We are changed forever. You were such an exceptional human being that I can't help but think if you could die at twenty-five, what hope is there for the rest of us?

Your love is the only answer I could come up with. What love and how?

Your love for your family and friends, nature, mountains, and a stable climate that makes joyful life possible is the love I mean, and the love we need. However, it is not sufficient that only those that knew you and loved you change but that humanity changes.

You knew how our love for nature and loved ones could save us through choices we make every day. These were habits you embraced; I know. Many millions more human beings need to adopt these behaviors, particularly those humans that consume the most.

Diet and cars just scratch the surface, as important as these areas are. The book I am writing will cover many more areas—energy, housing, and agriculture—to name just three. The idea remains the same: how love can save humanity and nature from pollution and climate apocalypse.

What loving acts preserve our planet so that we can live on more joyfully than in misery? How you led your life is my guide to a better future for us all.

I share my grief to cope but also to help others grieve, and then act. You would have liked that I channel my tragedy to help others as I move forward. Through this letter I make a link between climate and human grief, how they are alike and how they are different.

Soon after you died, I had a dream of you. You were walking away from me. I followed you and suddenly you turned around and silently gave me the biggest hug I remember you ever giving me. I woke up your arms still around me, slipping away into the darkness.

I will love you always,

Dad

What's left

Dust
Bright joyful memories
Four of us
Love, nightmares and dreams
Sadness, sleeplessness, solitude
Fear

A messed-up world!
Danger, egos, greed
War and hatred
Hopelessness

A hundred lives forever changed
Journeys without you
The past not the future
Broken hearts
Disappearing nature, glaciers
Grief

Nature reborn
All we can save
Writing
Hope
Joy and Laughter?
LOVE! AMOR! AMOUR!

Poems

Alex

Shy, humble and quiet laughter
Athletic wiry frame topped by a mop of hair
Impish grin that lit up your face
You brought us together and made us feel good
Your white snowman, green hat, orange nose, now alone

Son

Gone

Fire
Where are you?
Orange, hazy sky.
Talk of scones, cream and jam, your favorite
Never back
The rising pain, forever

Water
Thrashing in the dark, alone.
Why did you go?
The rain fills you and empties my heart
I loved you so

Landslide
Why did I let you go?
"It was safe, I know what I am doing, I will explain later"
You never could

Air
Your eyes above the oxygen mask, fear.
Life leaking, lost

All our other children
No, no, no!

Love

Tingle in your heart, heart ache
Mother's embrace
Safe as houses
Sharing life
In nature and of nature
Tender touch skin to skin
Within each other, accomplices
Blinding, forgiving and caring.
Spoken and unspoken

Grief

I see you
It's me on the floor
Wailing, thumping the ground
Shouting my disbelief and anger

My grief
Friend or foe?
Cutting at heart and mind
My companion forever, tend me or else!

Acknowledgments

To Deirdre for being such an amazing, loving mother and wife.

To Deirdre, Nicholas, and Emeline, heartbroken, together in grief and love.

To my mother Marichu, your love, "kitchen psychology" and profound empathy saves us. You put your own grief aside to help others grieve.

To my brother Martin. Like our father Gerry not a man of many words. What you said in Hondarribia about Alex was filled with so much love.

To my Irish and Spanish cousins, to Alex's cousins. Being able to see you and share the grief with you is a balm to my heart. To Isabel for her beautiful poem, and to Boom for inspiring her.

To Debby, my sister-in-law, for all your love.

To Duncan and Lindsey for holding us.

To Ingrid, my human shield.

To Anita, my editor, for helping me "put myself on to the page", Polly for encouraging me to write "from the heart", Adam to "click down 2 levels". To Erik for proofreading, your input on structure and how to "disentangle two octopuses". To Mark, Mike, Pietro, Roland, and many others who encouraged me to write.

To Oskar for his beautiful photograph on the front cover.

To Adam, Alberto, Alison, Enrico, Fred, Francesca, Ingrid, Kristen, and Weyn for hosting me in your homes and sharing your grief.

To all our dear friends and Alex's friends, not mentioned by name, with whom we share the pain, grief, love, and sorrow.

To Cheryl, Keri, Marsha, and Nadine who shared their precious and beautiful pieces at the writers' workshop in Maine last summer, led by our inspiring Anita.

To Sarah from Climate Solutions Switzerland, Elise from Climate and Sustainability, Markus, Patrick, and Philippe from Climate Endowment for your support and understanding.

JM, on a TGV (high-speed) train somewhere in South-West France.

October 26, 2022

About the Author

John Moorhead-Guinea is the author of *52 Solar Panels: Love and Grief for a Son and a Planet*, which reframes the argument for urgent behavior change to one of love, for yourself, your family, and the planet.

Moorhead-Guinea advocates for regenerative climate solutions that work in harmony with nature and prevent pollution. He is a founder of Climate Solutions Switzerland, Climate Action Accelerator, and an advisory board member of Climate and Sustainability. His career spans over 30 years in impact finance, coaching, consulting, and management. Moorhead-Guinea holds degrees from Geneva School of Business Administration (DAS), IE Business School (MBA), and Cambridge University (MA) in Natural Sciences. He lives in Le Châble, Switzerland with his family.

Printed by Amazon Italia Logistica S.r.l.
Torrazza Piemonte (TO), Italy